Transforming Conflict
Building Productive Relationships through Negotiation

Yvonne Marilyn James

Table of Contents

1. Introduction ... 2
2. Understanding the Nature of Conflict ... 3
   - 2.1. Understanding the Roots of Conflict ... 3
   - 2.2. A Profound Examination of The Types of Conflict ... 3
   - 2.3. The Stages of Conflict: From Latent to Aftermath ... 4
   - 2.4. How Perceptions and Expectations Fuel Conflict ... 5
   - 2.5. Conclusion ... 5
3. Fundamentals of Negotiation ... 6
   - 3.1. The Importance of Preparation ... 6
   - 3.2. The Negotiation Process ... 7
   - 3.3. Communication: The Heart of Negotiation ... 7
   - 3.4. Negotiating Styles ... 8
   - 3.5. The Role of Emotions ... 8
   - 3.6. Ethical Considerations ... 9
4. Effective Communication: More Than Just Words ... 10
   - 4.1. The Concept of Effective Communication ... 10
   - 4.2. The Role of Effective Communication in Negotiation ... 11
   - 4.3. Strategies to Enhance Communication Effectiveness ... 11
   - 4.4. Real-World Application: Communication Techniques for Negotiators ... 12
   - 4.5. Navigating Barriers in Effective Communication ... 13
5. Interpreting Non-Verbal Signals in Negotiation ... 14
6. The Art of Listening in Conflict Resolution ... 17
   - 6.1. Genuine Listening: More Than Just Hearing ... 17
   - 6.2. The Power of Empathetic Listening ... 17
   - 6.3. Active Listening and Effective Conflict Resolution ... 18
   - 6.4. Non-Verbal Signals in Listening ... 18
   - 6.5. The Challenges to Effective Listening ... 19

- 6.6. Attuning to the Hidden Messages 19
- 6.7. Conclusion: Turning Listening into a Strategic Tool 19
- 7. Strategies for Mutual Benefit: Establishing Win-Win Scenarios .. 21
  - 7.1. Framing Your Win-Win Objectives 21
  - 7.2. The Principle of Reciprocity 21
  - 7.3. Exploring Hidden Interests 22
  - 7.4. Utilising the BATNA 22
  - 7.5. Expanding the Pie 22
  - 7.6. Embracing Collaboration through Active Listening 23
  - 7.7. Managing Emotions 23
  - 7.8. Navigating Power Dynamics 23
- 8. Emotion Control: Maintaining Composure Under Pressure 25
  - 8.1. Understanding Emotional Responses 25
  - 8.2. Finding Your Emotional Triggers 26
  - 8.3. Emotion Regulation Techniques 26
  - 8.4. Building Emotional Resilience 27
  - 8.5. Applications in Actual Negotiations 27
- 9. Overcoming Barriers to Successful Negotiation 28
  - 9.1. Understanding the Barriers to Negotiation 28
  - 9.2. Preparatory Work: The Bedrock of Successful Negotiation .. 28
  - 9.3. Communication: The Lifeblood of Negotiation 29
  - 9.4. The Play of Power and its Impact 29
  - 9.5. Emotional Management: Key to Maintaining a Productive Climate 30
  - 9.6. Cognitive Biases: Silent Saboteurs 30
- 10. Case Studies: Successful Conflict Transformation through Negotiation 32
  - 10.1. Study 1: Successful Mitigation of a Business Dispute 32
  - 10.2. Study 2: Transformational Mediation in a Family Dispute .. 33
  - 10.3. Study 3: Resolution of an International Diplomatic Crisis .. 34

11. Future Directions: Continuing Your Negotiation and Conflict Resolution Journey 36
    11.1. Finding Your Negotiation Style 36
    11.2. Improvisation Through Practice 37
    11.3. Continuous Learning 37
    11.4. Refreshing Your Emotional Intelligence 37
    11.5. Exploring Mediation 38

Negotiation in the classic diplomatic sense assumes parties more anxious to agree than to disagree.

— Dean Acheson

Chapter 1. Introduction

In this Special Report, we dive into the fascinating world of "Transforming Conflict: Building Productive Relationships through Negotiation". Trade misunderstanding and tension for connection and harmony as we guide you through the vast landscape of negotiation tactics. Discover how effective communication can turn even the most antagonistic relationships into productive alliances. No technical jargon here, just simple, practical and engaging strategies to enhance your bargaining skills. Galvanizing and insightful, this report is specifically tailored to provide you with tools that will turn challenging conflicts into win-win situations. Read on, and let's embark on this transformative journey together to leverage the power of negotiation, rejuvenate relationships, and achieve outstanding results. The value contained within these pages is too fruitful to pass up – secure your copy of the report today!

Chapter 2. Understanding the Nature of Conflict

Every journey, no matter how enriching, begins with the first step, which might as well be the most crucial. Understanding the nature of conflict is that critical first stride on a path to mastering negotiation and conflict resolution skills. This chapter will uncover the roots of conflict, the types and stages of conflict, and the role of perceptions and expectations in fueling disputes. Armed with this informed perspective, you will be better equipped to maneuver your way around points of contention and harness the transformative power of negotiation.

2.1. Understanding the Roots of Conflict

Conflict is as old as humanity itself. The origin of conflict emerges from differences, be it in opinions, motivations, perceptions, values, or desires. These differences can lead to a clash of interests, thereby giving birth to conflict.

While often perceived in a negative light, conflict is not inherently bad. If managed appropriately, it can stimulate growth, facilitate change, inspire creativity, and lead to better decision making. However, to harness these potential benefits, it's crucial we first understand the root of these clashes.

2.2. A Profound Examination of The Types of Conflict

Broadly, conflicts can be segmented into two categories: intrinsic and extrinsic. Intrinsic conflicts originate from the inside, fueled by our personal values, beliefs, and emotions. Opposite to it, extrinsic conflicts arise from the external world and revolve around tangible issues like resources, time, or practices. Sometimes, the extrinsic conflicts might actually be a manifestation of the intrinsic ones.

It's also beneficial to categorize conflicts depending on the individuals or groups involved. In this regard, we have intrapersonal conflict (a conflict within oneself), interpersonal conflict (conflict between individuals), intragroup conflict (conflict within a group), and intergroup conflict (conflict between groups). Recognizing the type of conflict you are dealing with is the first step to managing it effectively.

2.3. The Stages of Conflict: From Latent to Aftermath

Conflict is not an abrupt phenomenon; it follows specific stages, from latent to aftermath. Each stage has its own dynamics and requires unique strategies for effective resolution.

1. Latent stage: This is the stage where potential for conflict exists due to underlying differences, but it has not yet manifested.
2. Perceived stage: Here, the parties involve start to perceive the conflict, although no overt clash has happened yet.
3. Felt stage: At this stage, parties begin to emotionally react to the conflict; stress and anxiety may start building up.
4. Manifest stage: This is where the conflict becomes open, and disagreements are expressed. This stage is most recognizable as "conflict".
5. Aftermath stage: This final stage deals with the consequences of the conflict, which could be positive or negative, depending upon how it was managed.

Each stage of conflict provides us with an opportunity to respond or intervene effectively, thereby influencing the trajectory of the conflict.

2.4. How Perceptions and Expectations Fuel Conflict

Perception is our way of making sense of the world around us. Our perceptions, however, are influenced by numerous factors, and so they often differ from person to person. Conflicts can arise when there is a gap between the perception of an individual and the actual reality.

Similarly, expectations can set the stage for conflict. Each individual or group enters a negotiation with a set of expectations. When these expectations don't align, or when they are not met, conflict can ensue. For effective conflict resolution, it is crucial to recognize and manage these gaps in perceptions and expectations.

2.5. Conclusion

With a comprehensive understanding of the nature of conflict, we are now better equipped to navigate our way through any disagreement or dispute. This chapter forms the foundation for the chapters to follow, which will dive deeper into the practical strategies and techniques for conflict resolution using effective negotiation skills.

Let's move forward in our journey and explore the next chapter - 'Fundamentals of Negotiation', where we will discover the principles that underpin successful negotiation.

Chapter 3. Fundamentals of Negotiation

Before we dive into the distinct elements of negotiation, let's take a step back and establish what negotiation is fundamentally. At its core, negotiation is a process through which two or more parties, each with their own aims, needs, and viewpoints, try to find common ground to reach an agreement for mutual benefit. The agreement aims to resolve points of conflict, leveraging the power of discourse, persuasion, and compromise to shape a resolution that all parties can accept.

3.1. The Importance of Preparation

Arguably the most critical phase of any negotiation, preparation is the cornerstone upon which successful negotiations are built. The preparation stage involves understanding the bargaining landscape fully. This includes a comprehensive evaluation of your own standpoints, your firm points, and potential flexibility areas, as well as the same for your negotiation counterpart.

Essential aspects encompass setting clear objectives, ascertaining BATNA (Best Alternative To a Negotiated Agreement), and researching your negotiating counterpart's potential needs and objectives. Keep in mind that your BATNA is your power tool. It provides a yard measure of how low you are willing to go and serves as a contingency plan should negotiations reach a stalemate.

For a successful negotiator, no detail is too small. You must strive to identify all the potential issues that would arise during the negotiation and anticipate possible rebuttals and objections.

3.2. The Negotiation Process

Understanding the negotiation process can equip you with the strategic and tactical knowledge to navigate the negotiation landscape. This process typically unfolds over five stages:

1. Rapport Building
2. Issue Identification
3. Bargaining
4. Conclusion Drawing
5. Agreement and Implementation

Rapport building is the foundation of trust. It involves creating a friendly atmosphere and finding common ground with your counterpart. The next stage, issue identification, involves each party stating their cases, concerns, and wants. During the bargaining stage, parties reveal their offers, counteroffers, and concessions. After this, conclusion drawing entails making final offers, analyzing options, and deciding on the bargaining's final outcome. Finally, Agreement and Implementation : This is when the negotiated outcomes are put into action after agreeing on the specific terms and conditions.

3.3. Communication: The Heart of Negotiation

The art of successful negotiation is primarily the art of effective communication. Providing clear, concise, and focused messages ensures that all parties are aligned in their understanding. Verbal and non-verbal cues both play a significant role in shaping the trajectory of a negotiation. Mastering the ability to read and respond to these cues can give you a definitive edge.

3.4. Negotiating Styles

There exists an array of negotiating styles, each with its advantages and potential pitfalls. The primary ones include competitive, collaborative, compromise, avoidance, and accommodating. The choice of style often depends upon the nature of the negotiation, the relationship between the parties, and their respective individual personalities.

Competitive style is assertiveness personified. It entails a clear focus on achieving personal outcomes, even at the expense of the other party's needs. A collaborative style calls for a more empathetic approach, focusing on win-win outcomes and value creation for both sides. On the other side is the compromising style, when negotiators strive for a quick middle-ground solution.

Avoidance implies a reluctance to engage in the negotiation process, often due to fear of conflict or lacking confidence in negotiation skills. Lastly, the accommodating style sees negotiators willingly making concessions to maintain positive relationships at the expense of their own needs and objectives.

3.5. The Role of Emotions

Emotions can be a double-edged sword during negotiations. On one hand, displaying too much emotion may be viewed as weakness and can be exploited by a crafty negotiator. On the other, an absence of emotions can make one seem overly rigid or uncaring, potentially stifling rapport building efforts.

Successful negotiators must strike a balance: managing and controlling their own emotions while being mindful of the emotional cues of their counterparts. This emotional intelligence is a crucial factor that can enhance the effectiveness of one's negotiation tactics.

3.6. Ethical Considerations

Ethics play a vital role in negotiation. Fairness, honesty, and integrity are not just moral imperatives, but they are intrinsic to securing sustainable and long-lasting agreement outcomes. Remember, 'winning' a negotiation by deceit might grant short-term gains, but it can erode trust and hamstring future negotiations.

There's no one-size-fits-all approach to negotiation. A masterful negotiator pays attention to all the nuanced layers pertaining to their approach to negotiation, their communication style, their emotional management, and ethical considerations. Through this chapter, you are now familiar with the fundamental building blocks of this artful process known as negotiation. Armed with this knowledge, you're well on your way to transforming conflict and building productive relationships.

Chapter 4. Effective Communication: More Than Just Words

At the heart of conflict transformation is the art and science of effective communication. A truly effective communication is one that speaks more than just words, that reaches the heart of the receiver as if those words are innate and already understood. This chapter offers a comprehensive exploration of such type of communication – deep, profound, influential – and its invaluable role in negotiation.

4.1. The Concept of Effective Communication

We begin with an in-depth understanding of what effective communication encapsulates. This important concept refers to the process of transferring information from one person to another in a manner that it can be understood, absorbed, and later utilized by the receiver. It's more than mere exchange of words; it's about sharing ideas, emotions, directions, and several other impressionable aspects of human interaction.

Effective communication takes into account two key factors: message and medium. The message should be clear, concise, and complete, and the medium chosen should be appropriate to the situation and the individuals involved. In negotiation settings, the message and medium of communication must be such that the outcome is mutually satisfying, progressive and enduring.

4.2. The Role of Effective Communication in Negotiation

Effective communication enables us to express ourselves, understand others, and bring about meaningful exchanges. In the realm of negotiation, it plays a pivotal role in shaping outcomes, cultivating trust, and nurturing rewarding relationships. It helps in letting go of the past grudges, overcoming miscommunications and unearthing common ground.

Sound negotiation strategies rely heavily on effective communication. Agreeing and disagreeing, gathering and scrutinizing information, influencing and persuading – all involve communication at their core. Rules of engagement, setting negotiation climate, separators and deal makers - they all are tied intrinsically with how effectively the negotiators communicate.

It is through effective communication that we express our positions, understand the needs of others, and explore potential compromises. And especially in conflict situations, it allows participants to navigate tension and uncover pathways to transform it into win-win scenarios.

4.3. Strategies to Enhance Communication Effectiveness

We can adopt several strategies to enhance communication effectiveness.

1. Clarity: Be clear about what you want to communicate. Use simple language and avoid jargon.
2. Listen Actively: Show genuine interest in other's viewpoints. Remember, listening is a crucial aspect of communication.

3. Respond, Don't React: Responding requires thinking and understanding, whereas a reaction is usually instinctive and often diminishes communication effectiveness.
4. Control Emotions: Keep your emotions in check. Emotional outbursts can cloud judgement and hinder level-headed communication.
5. Non-Verbal Communication: Pay attention to your non-verbal cues like body language, tone of voice, eye contact, etc., as they can reinforce or contradict your words.

4.4. Real-World Application: Communication Techniques for Negotiators

In practical terms, negotiation scenarios call for certain specific communication techniques. Here are some that experts swear by:

- Asking Open-Ended Questions: By doing this, you invite the counterpart to share additional information, prompting a deeper conversation.
- Mirroring: This is the practice of subtly mimicking another person's language or behavior, creating rapport and cultivating trust.
- Framing: Framing is presenting information in a way that influences how it is received. It can be used to shape perceptions and steer the negotiation in your desired direction.
- Summarizing and Paraphrasing: This provides a confirmation that the conveyed message is understood correctly, reducing chances of misunderstanding.

Each of these techniques can provide a competitive edge in a negotiation scenario, lending to the artistry in transformative conflict resolution. By acknowledging the power inherent in effective communication, we can bring about deep and productive exchanges – it really is more than just words.

4.5. Navigating Barriers in Effective Communication

Just as valuable it is to master effective communication techniques, it's equally important to recognize and overcome communication barriers. Common barriers include cultural differences, language barriers, cognitive biases, emotional responses, and misunderstood non-verbal cues.

Acknowledging these barriers and implementing strategies to counteract them can facilitate seamless and meaningful engagement during negotiation processes. This requires empathy, the ability to reflect, the humility to learn and change, and the courage to address the elephant in the room.

As we close this journey through the art of communicating effectively in negotiation, let us remember that mastering this skill arms us with a powerful tool, opening doors to understanding, building bridges over conflicts, and reaching the shores of productive relationships. Let every word you say and every gesture you make add value to the conversation at hand and lighten the path of resolution.

Chapter 5. Interpreting Non-Verbal Signals in Negotiation

\=== Understanding Non-Verbal Communication

The power of non-verbal communication cannot be underestimated—indeed, numerous studies have shown that it forms a significant part of how we understand and interpret the actions of others. Non-verbal communication ranges from facial expressions, body language, voice tonality and even something as subtle as breathing.

According to the famous psychologist Albert Mehrabian, words only account for a small percentage of the overall message in any face-to-face conversation—about 7%. The rest is communicated through non-verbal cues such as tone of voice (38%) and body language (55%). This makes it indispensable to understand and analyze these non-verbal signals to enhance negotiation effectiveness.

\=== Deconstructing Facial Expressions

Facial expressions are one of the most subconscious yet most telling aspects of non-verbal communication. Micro-expressions, fleeting displays of emotion lasting only a fraction of a second, can reveal genuine emotions even when someone is attempting to conceal them.

For instance, a sudden tightening of the jaw may suggest anger or annoyance, a brief lift of the eyebrows could indicate surprise or skepticism, and pupil dilation is often associated with interest or excitement. Being aware of these nuanced indications can provide a wealth of insight in negotiations, potentially alerting you to inconsistencies between what your counterpart is saying and how they truly feel.

\=== Body Language Insights

Body language, or kinesics, is a rich source of information about a person's attitudes and feelings. A person leaning forward might show genuine interest, commitment, or aggression, while crossed arms could symbolize defensiveness or disinterest. However, caution must be taken to note cultural variations because what might be deemed as a sign of disinterest in one culture might be indicative of respect in another.

In negotiation, understanding these clues can help adjust the course of conversation, giving indications on when to press ahead, or when it's time to step back and consider a different approach.

\=== Voice Tonality and Its Impact

The tonality of a person's voice carries weight in revealing one's inner emotions and viewpoints. A hurried or excited tone could suggest eagerness or panic, while a lower tone might denote seriousness or authority. Pauses may indicate thoughtfulness or uncertainty. A suave negotiator must be adept in "listening between the words," hearing not only what is being said, but how it's being said. The volume, pitch, and speed of speech all hold nuanced clues to a speaker's mindset and emotional state.

\=== Interpreting Breathing Patterns

While often overlooked, breathing patterns can be instrumental in decoding the emotional status of an individual. For example, shallow, quick breaths could symbolize stress or discomfort, whereas slow, deep breaths usually indicate a calm or relaxed state. In negotiations, being attuned to shifts in breathing can alert you to changes in the internal state of the other party, providing additional insight into how they're responding to the discussion and what their true feelings have been.

\=== Importance of Context in Interpreting Non-Verbal Signals

Although understanding individual signals is vital when interpreting non-verbal cues, the context within which these gestures, expressions or tones are observed is just as crucial. Each element of non-verbal communication does not exist in isolation. Cross-referencing and analyzing these signals in their total context will yield the most accurate interpretation.

\=== Enhancing Your Own Non-Verbal Communication Skills

Understanding non-verbal communication also means being aware of your own. Your bodily actions, facial expressions, tone of voice, and even breathing patterns are all under constant scrutiny in a negotiation setting. Cultivating a bodily language that exudes confidence, openness, and sincerity can significantly influence the direction of the negotiation in your favor.

In conclusion, interpreting non-verbal signals in negotiation is an intricate process involving precise perception, acute observation, and practiced understanding of various cues and patterns. Non-verbal signals provide a deeper dimension to the communication process in a negotiation, revealing hidden emotions, attitudes, and intents. Mastering the understanding and usage of these signals can inherently enrich the complexity and success of your negotiation skills.

Chapter 6. The Art of Listening in Conflict Resolution

In the pursuit of conflict resolution through negotiation, the art of listening arises as a core competency, a pillar upon which the edifice of productive exchange is built. It involves more than just perceiving the words that are spoken; it demands in-depth understanding, empathy, and analytical interpretation skills.

6.1. Genuine Listening: More Than Just Hearing

Close attention to the speaker's words is, of course, key, but authentic listening goes beyond that. It encompasses not just what is said, but also how it's said, and what is left unsaid. The tone, pace, volume, and inflection - each element carries a message. A raised voice may suggest frustration or urgency, while a quieter tone could signal reticence or contemplation.

Moreover, genuine listening respects the silence, without rushing to fill it. Silence facilitates introspection, and can often lead to greater clarity in thought and expression. Demonstrating patience in these silent moments is also a testament to one's respect for the speaker.

6.2. The Power of Empathetic Listening

Empathetic listening isn't confined merely to understanding the speaker's expressed ideas, but extends to understanding their thoughts, feelings, and intentions. It means stepping into their shoes, immersing oneself in the speaker's perspective and conveying that this perspective is valued and acknowledged.

Empathy dissolves barriers that exist in discussions, promoting a sense of connection and collaboration. By echoing the sentiments and reflecting the feelings, the listener shows their commitment to joint resolution.

6.3. Active Listening and Effective Conflict Resolution

Active listening is an engaged process, demanding more than mere attentiveness. It includes reflecting back to the speaker with paraphrasing to display comprehension, asking clarifying questions, summarizing the speaker's thoughts and affirming their sentiments. This back-and-forth promotes understanding and signifies respect for the speaker's viewpoint.

Active listening elicits openness from both parties, which enhances transparency, encourages truthful discussions, and fosters an environment conducive for productive negotiation.

6.4. Non-Verbal Signals in Listening

Cues observed in body language, facial expressions, and eye contact are also vital components of listening. Maintaining eye contact and demonstrating engaged body language are essential to establish trust and openness. Meanwhile, reading the other party's non-verbal signs can provide insights into their thoughts and feelings, which might not be verbally expressed.

6.5. The Challenges to Effective Listening

In any negotiation, barriers can impede effective listening. Distractions, bias, prejudgments, and over-reliance on the spoken word can all present hurdles. Overcoming these challenges requires self-awareness, discipline, and practice. By acknowledging and addressing these barriers, one can enhance their listening skills, thereby aiding conflict resolution.

6.6. Attuning to the Hidden Messages

Listening extends beyond the oral exchange to include the 'messages between the lines.' This involves recognizing the subtext, unspoken sentiments, or hidden frustrations that could be impacting the conversation. Sensing these underlying currents enables the listener to address any brewing tension, and bring the dialogue back on track.

6.7. Conclusion: Turning Listening into a Strategic Tool

The art of listening is a strategic tool that can elevate the outcome of any negotiation or conflict resolution process. Its skillful deployment not only builds trust and understanding between parties but can also provide valuable insights to strategize and navigate the path to conflict resolution.

The journey of honing listening skills is gradual, but rewarding, whereby one grows not just as a negotiator but also as a compassionate and understanding individual.

In sum, the art of listening provides a foundational stone upon which conflict resolution can be constructively built. By harnessing the principles of genuine understanding, empathy, active participation, non-verbal signal interpretation, and subtext perception, the listener wields a potent tool to facilitate the transformation from conflict to negotiation, from stand-off to understanding, and culminating in a win-win resolution. Through persistent practice and mindful application of these principles, the labyrinth of conflict can be effectively negotiated, leading to more productive and harmonious outcomes.

Chapter 7. Strategies for Mutual Benefit: Establishing Win-Win Scenarios

To ensure a comprehensive understanding, we would embark on this remarkable expedition by first establishing a universal truth: that everyone involved in a negotiation desires an outcome that benefits them. Hence, the objective of the 'win-win scenarios' is to strive relentlessly towards an agreement where all participating parties leave the table feeling satisfied.

7.1. Framing Your Win-Win Objectives

Framing denotes the process of defining the negotiation's context or perspective. It's comparable to delineating a portrait and deciding on the picture's elements to emphasize or downplay. A powerful frame focuses on mutual benefits and fosters collaboration.

Avoid castigating your position into a rigid one, but rather show flexibility in order to allow for creative problem-solving strategies. By viewing the negotiation as a challenge to unravel together rather than a combat, we promote a more cooperative environment that favors establishing win-win scenarios.

7.2. The Principle of Reciprocity

Reciprocity – referring to our inherent human drive to repay what's given to us – is a potent negotiation tool that can guide our conversation towards win-win scenarios. To do so, you might consider offering an initial concession, a gesture of goodwill to encourage the other party to reciprocate.

However, it's imperative to strike a balance. You must avoid making hasty concessions that could potentially weaken your bargaining position. Aim at gradual mutual concessions that ease the deadlock and push towards a shared agreement.

7.3. Exploring Hidden Interests

Oftentimes, negotiation interests hide like unseen currents beneath the water's surface. They dictate the direction of the negotiation, yet remain unspoken. Diving deep and discerning these hidden interests could pave the route to a win-win resolution. Understand that interests are needs, desires, fears or concerns that are at the heart of the matter and not always as simple as monetary value.

Unmask these quiet influencers, find common grounds or shared interests for mutual benefits, and weave them into your negotiation fabric.

7.4. Utilising the BATNA

Your Best Alternative To a Negotiated Agreement (BATNA) serves as your ace in the hole, a strong fallback should the negotiation grind to a frustrating halt. Identifying it allows you to gauge the lower limit of your willingness to accept a deal, hence providing you with increased negotiation power. Simultaneously, strive to understand the opposing party's BATNA.

7.5. Expanding the Pie

Negotiations tend to have a reputation for being a zero-sum game – one person's gain equates to the other's loss. Yet, this belief is outdated and limits potential outcomes. Instead, shift toward a paradigm of value creation, often coined as 'expanding the pie'.

In this, aim to generate as many options and alternatives as possible, without prematurely judging them. This expands the pool of resources for negotiation and allows for opportunities to satisfy various interests of all parties involved.

7.6. Embracing Collaboration through Active Listening

Active listening is an essential ingredient to unlock win-win scenarios as it allows you to fully understand the other party's perspective and anticipate accordingly. It emphasizes on showing empathy and validating the opposite party's views, hence fostering a cooperative spirit.

7.7. Managing Emotions

Effective negotiation is rarely devoid of emotions. They can either fuel the fire of discord or be channels leading to a shared understanding. Emotion management ensures the latter. Understand your triggers and maintain composure to avoid clouding decision-making processes.

7.8. Navigating Power Dynamics

Finally, power dynamics wield considerable influence in negotiation. It's crucial to understand and navigate them wisely. Focus on enhancing your power, without manipulating or exploiting the other party. Equipped with earned respect and charisma, power can be used to drive the negotiation towards a win-win agreement.

In conclusion, creating win-win scenarios, though challenging, is achievable by focusing on mutual benefit, exploring hidden interests, using BATNA wisely, expanding the potential 'pie', managing emotions, and navigating power dynamics effectively. Engaging these strategies will undoubtedly lead your negotiation journey towards successful resolutions and thriving relationships.

Chapter 8. Emotion Control: Maintaining Composure Under Pressure

In the thrumming crux of high-stakes negotiation, emotions often dart out from the shadows: frustration tickling the back of your neck, impatience grinding the gears of your mind, perhaps even the icy tickle of fear. Yet, the ability to maintain composure under the pressure cooker of negotiation – that is a skill that separates the effective negotiators from the rest. It's the indispensable art of emotion control. Mastery of this quality fine-tunes your presence, sharpens your decision-making, and increases the likelihood of achieving preferred outcomes, even in amidst choppy conflict seas.

8.1. Understanding Emotional Responses

In the primal soup of human cognition, neuroscientists tell us that two types of thinking exist: fast and slow. Fast thinking is instinctual, reactive, forged in the blistering heat of survival necessities. Slow thinking, on the other hand, is deliberate, calculated, thoughtful. When thrown into stressful situations, our cognition tends to default to the efficient, though simplistic, fast thinking. In this immediacy, emotions seize control of our actions. This can lead to the heat-of-the-moment decisions that may harm the negotiation process and sabotage the possibility of a win-win outcome. Understanding this relationship between stress and emotional responses is the first step towards emotion control.

8.2. Finding Your Emotional Triggers

Self-awareness is a cornerstone in conflict resolution and negotiation. To manage one's emotions, we first need to recognize what ignites them. Think back to past negotiations; what made your blood boil or heart race? Recognize that these triggers exist, then examine them. Understanding why they exist can unravel the hold they have over your reactions. By identifying these triggers, you can foster a sense of predictability about your emotional reactions, thereby providing a platform for control.

8.3. Emotion Regulation Techniques

Managing emotional responses isn't about suppressing them; it's about regulating them to enrich your negotiation performance. A handful of strategies can prove beneficial, each requiring consistent practice and dedication for perfection.

Deep Breathing: Combat the rapid heartbeat and shallow breathing of stress with deep, controlled breaths. This signals to your body that the danger is averted, thereby soothing the panicked flight-or-fight response.

Mindfulness: Embrace the present. Instead of being swept up in what-if scenarios, ground your awareness in the here and now. Notice the texture of the table, the taste of the water, the air stirring in the room. Such attentiveness can create a tranquil mental space, cushioning you from the turbulence of emotional unrest.

Reframing: Try viewing the situation from a different perspective. This exercise forces slow, deliberate thinking and provides a broader understanding of the scenario. It aids you in dissociating personal feelings from the realities of the negotiation, fostering a level-headed environment for decision-making.

8.4. Building Emotional Resilience

Strength isn't just in the power of your arguments or the size of your concessions, it's also in your capacity to bounce back from emotional jabs. Tolerance for adversity, or resilience, is what allows you to dust off after a setback without surrendering to emotional turbulence. Building emotional resilience might include expanding your stress tolerance, enhancing your problem-solving skills, or finding social support networks to buffer stress during negotiations. These combined efforts equip you with the necessary protection against emotionally taxing negotiation scenarios.

8.5. Applications in Actual Negotiations

At its core, effective negotiation is as much about combating internal, self-imposed challenges as it is about navigating external conflicts. Incorporating these tools into your negotiation protocol can bring poise and stability to your negotiation dynamics, thus enabling better decision-making and delivering favorable outcomes. The presence of mind that emotional regulation supplies allows you to face negotiation challenges with billowing courage instead of dwindling impulse.

When it comes to controlling emotions under pressure, there's no magic potion or quick fix. It's a talent to be honed, a muscle to be strengthened. Each failed negotiation, every heated argument, is but a stepping-stone in this transformative journey to master the art of maintaining composure under pressure. Embrace the process and watch as your negotiation prowess expands, bolstered by your newfound ability to stay calm amidst the storm.

Chapter 9. Overcoming Barriers to Successful Negotiation

Achieving successful negotiations can often seem like a Herculean task, owing to the various barriers that must be overcome. These barriers may range from psychological to logistical to communication-based, each demanding its own unique approach to resolution. Let's start with an in-depth understanding of these barriers and journey together through the wide array of strategies to overcome them effectively.

9.1. Understanding the Barriers to Negotiation

Barriers to successful negotiation can span across a diverse spectrum. At times, it encompasses everything from personal factors, such as cognitive biases and emotional baggage, to broader relational and structural issues. There's a raft of such barriers that can hamper the negotiation process, which include but are not limited to - Lack of Preparation, Communication Issues, Power Dynamics, Unmanaged Emotions, and Cognitive Biases. We will investigate each of these areas in detail as we proceed through this chapter, with the objective of equipping you with effective and practical tools to surmount these barriers.

9.2. Preparatory Work: The Bedrock of Successful Negotiation

The importance of preparing is not lost on most people, yet it remains a consistently underutilized part of the negotiation process.

Preparation isn't just about examining potential outcomes or responses, it's about seeing the entire picture. It involves identifying the objectives, potential tactics, factors influencing the negotiation, and the interests of the other party. Being unprepared is akin to navigating through uncharted territory without a map. The shortcut to overcoming this barrier is developing a clear strategy, conducting thorough research, understanding the context, and being aware of the interests, fears, and concerns of the other side.

9.3. Communication: The Lifeblood of Negotiation

Though it may seem self-evident, the lack of open, effective, and respectful communication can often transform potential collaborations into irreparable impasses. This barrier springs from misconceptions, misinterpretations, and mistrust coupled with a lack of active listening skills. To overcome such hindrances, it's imperative to convey your thoughts explicitly, seek clarification when confused, use simple and clear language, pay heed to the non-verbal cues, and to always listen with the intent to understand rather than answer.

9.4. The Play of Power and its Impact

Power dynamics can significantly influence the progress and the outcome of any negotiation. The perception of power can sometimes inhibit the free exchange of ideas and limit collaborative solutions. Uneven playing fields can leave one party feeling bullied or disadvantaged, leading to a less than satisfactory resolution. To transcend such barriers, try shifting the focus from positional power to the power of arguments, ideas, and solutions. Understanding and accepting the power dynamics can help in devising strategies to counteract those influences, making interactions more balanced and advantageous for both parties.

9.5. Emotional Management: Key to Maintaining a Productive Climate

We are emotional beings, and conflict can often invite eruption of intense emotions. These emotions can cloud judgment, spur impulsive decisions, and escalate the conflict rather than resolve it. Managing emotions effectively requires building emotional intelligence, comprising self-awareness, self-regulation, empathy, and social skills. Self-awareness identifies emotional triggers, while self-regulation assists in keeping those emotions in check. Empathy facilitates the understanding of others' emotions, and social skills enable the expression of emotions in appropriate ways.

9.6. Cognitive Biases: Silent Saboteurs

Cognitive biases, the inherent quirks in our thinking and rationality that push us to make illogical decisions, can impede our understanding, interpretation, and perception of the negotiation process. Common cognitive biases like 'anchoring', 'overconfidence effect', 'confirmation bias', 'conservatism bias', 'availability bias' and 'endowment effect', can skew our negotiation outcomes unfavorably. The remedy lies in being aware of these biases, practicing objective thinking, verifying information, considering all possible options, and seeking feedback from trusted individuals.

In summary, overcoming barriers to successful negotiation involves a labyrinthian and often challenging path. However, with systematic understanding, thorough preparation, effective communication, the right balance of power, managing emotions adeptly and curbing cognitive biases, the road to successful negotiation becomes paved with realistic possibilities. The understanding and applications of these concepts and strategies, evidenced in the succeeding chapters, will empower you to transform your personal and professional conflicts, and to harness the energy within those conflicts to craft agreements satisfying the interests of all parties involved. Consequently, you'll witness a dramatic shift from conflicting interests and zero-sum disputes towards a mutual problem-solving approach, marking true progress in your negotiation and conflict resolution journey.

Chapter 10. Case Studies: Successful Conflict Transformation through Negotiation

We delve into our investigation of negotiation with a selection of illuminating case studies that illustrate the power and efficacy of conflict transformation. These stories, hailing from various arenas—business, personal relationships, and international diplomacy—underscore the critical role of negotiation in finding resolutions that not only meet conflicting parties' demands but also cultivate ensuing beneficial relationships.

10.1. Study 1: Successful Mitigation of a Business Dispute

Our first case takes us into the world of international business, involving a discord between two cutting-edge technological firms, hailing from the United States and Japan. The crux of the issue revolved around the dissatisfaction expressed by the Japanese firm over the deliverables provided by the American company. Instead of escalating the situation, the American company demonstrated a high level of negotiation competence, transforming the conflict into a potential sustainable alliance.

A detailed appraisal of the dilemma was the first step in the negotiation, revealing subtle communication errors and cultural misunderstandings. The American firm implemented active listening, showing genuine interest in comprehending the Japanese company's concerns. They also made a diligent effort to interpret their non-verbal signals which helped significantly in this predominantly high-context culture. The American company's chief negotiator, instead of employing a defensive strategy, allowed for an open dialogue where both parties could express their emotions and viewpoints.

Through maintaining a composed demeanor and paying heed to the interests of the Japanese firm, trust was gradually established, and a win-win situation was formulated. This situation provided a platform where both parties managed to refine their technical specifications, price, and terms of collaboration, leading to a mutually advantageous business relationship.

10.2. Study 2: Transformational Mediation in a Family Dispute

Our second case study navigates the turbulent seas of familial discord, showcasing how conflict can be successfully managed within close interpersonal relationships. The dispute arose between two siblings over the division of their late parents' estate. Both siblings felt strongly about keeping certain meaningful memorabilia and, as a result, were unwilling to compromise, leading to a stalemate.

A skilled mediator was brought in with the intention of forming open, non-confrontational dialogues. The mediator influenced the siblings to express their emotional attachments rather than adopt adversarial positions. This communicative approach allowed each sibling to respect the other's sentiments without feeling threatened.

The negotiation approach included active listening, non-verbal signals' interpretation, and maintaining composure despite the high tension. Gradually, there was a transition from a competitive to a cooperative orientation, and both siblings could see the benefits of a win-win solution. Instead of hegemonizing their interests, they started empathizing with each other and worked out a solution that secured their emotional peace, nurturing their bond in the process.

10.3. Study 3: Resolution of an International Diplomatic Crisis

Our final case takes us to the significant stage of international diplomacy, wherein two nations found themselves on opposite ends of a financial dispute. The conflict was based on the allegation by Country A that Country B failed to honor financial commitments in a joint infrastructure project, which led to significant losses for Country A.

Despite the stakes, the representatives of both countries agreed to partake in peace talks. The negotiators emphasized facilitating transparent communication, expressing their interests, and identifying a common ground for resolving the issue. Emotional control played a substantial role here, as heated exchanges could potentially cast severe ramifications on multi-layered international relations.

Understanding the gravity of the situation, both sides agreed to a renegotiation of the financial commitments. Further, a joint supervisory board was established to oversee future transactions and prevent similar misunderstandings. The win-win scenario helped soothe ruffled feathers, ensured smooth progress of the project, and bolstered mutual trust, establishing a robust foundation for future collaborations.

Taken together, these case studies underscore the transformative potential that negotiation holds in resolving conflicts. From mitigating business disputes to resolving personal relationship issues, and averting international crises, the principles of negotiation and conflict resolution are universal. When employed meticulously, these strategies have the power to dissolve tensions, catalyze cooperation, and foster shared prosperity, turning even the most insurmountable conflicts into opportunities for growth and collaboration.

These real-world examples offer substantial, practical insights for anyone seeking to refine their negotiation competency. As you continue your journey towards mastering this timeless art, remember that the crux of successful negotiation lies in establishing constructive communication, engaging in active listening, controlling emotions, and seeking mutually beneficial outcomes, thus transforming festering conflicts into beneficial alliances.

Chapter 11. Future Directions: Continuing Your Negotiation and Conflict Resolution Journey

Our journey into understanding and mastering conflict resolution through negotiation, much like any quest for learning, does not have an endpoint. Instead, it holds a continuum of sorts wherein the more we learn, adapt, and evolve, the more the horizon expands, proposing newer challenges and insights. In this closing chapter, we will explore the future steps you can take to continually refine your negotiation and conflict resolution skills, ultimately leading towards your evolution into a master strategist.

11.1. Finding Your Negotiation Style

Your negotiation style is akin to your unique fingerprint, a blend of conscious techniques and unconscious habits that you resort to within a negotiation setting. Understanding this unique style is pivotal to your developmental journey. While some may rely on aggressive techniques to seal the deal, others might use their affability and charm, and some could employ methodical problem-solving techniques.

Reflect on your past negotiations — be it an argument with a friend or a family member, or a high-stakes corporate deal — identify the recurring patterns, and try to distil your unique negotiation style. Once aware of your style, question it. Could I have been more assertive or empathetic? Could I have engaged more with the problem rather than attacking the person? This introspective evaluation will allow you to identify areas of improvement and evolve your negotiation tactics, aligning them better with your professional and personal objectives.

11.2. Improvisation Through Practice

Akin to virtuoso musicians, skilled negotiators are masters of improvisation. The secret to acquiring this adaptability is — consistent and mindful practice. Simulate negotiation scenarios, either by placing yourself in individually challenging situations or by organizing mock negotiations within your team. Actively seek out people and situations that challenge you and push you out of your comfort zones. This could mean negotiating with someone who communicates differently than you, or it could mean negotiating a subject matter that you're not particularly familiar with. Each negotiation encounter will expose you to a varied set of circumstances, helping you become more adaptive and confident.

11.3. Continuous Learning

Achieving mastery in negotiation doesn't come overnight, and it doesn't stop with mastering a set of techniques. Constantly update your knowledge pool by reading books, attending workshops, and regularly engaging in discussions on the subject. Discover new theories, case studies, and breakthroughs in the field which can give you fresh insights and refine your strategies. Widely celebrated works like 'Getting to Yes' by Fisher and Ury or 'Negotiation Genius' by Malhotra and Bazerman can serve as excellent starting points for this ongoing journey of learning.

11.4. Refreshing Your Emotional Intelligence

Emotional Intelligence (EI) is the underpinning fabric that coherently ties all aspects of negotiation together. It encapsulates empathy, emotion management, interpersonal relationships, and social awareness. Therefore, constantly updating and refreshing your understanding and application of EI is crucial. Reflect on your emotional responses in different negotiation scenarios—when did you react impulsively? When did you maintain composure even under high pressure? It's this ongoing journey of understanding, sense-making, applying, and reflecting on Emotional Intelligence that can fortify your negotiation skills and prepare you for complex conflict scenarios.

11.5. Exploring Mediation

Lastly, think about stepping into the shoes of a mediator. Mediation occurs when a impartial third party steps in to aid in resolving a dispute. By becoming a mediator, you can gain exposure to a wide range of conflict scenarios, enhance your empathetic understanding, strengthen your patience, and improve your ability to steer conversations towards mutually beneficial outcomes. You could consider taking a professional course in mediation, or offer to mediate the next time you encounter a disagreement within your personal or professional circles.

This chapter purposefully serves as an ending that doesn't close; a thread stretching out into your future, encouraging the application, reflection, and evolution of your negotiation skills. Remember, every conversation holds the potential to be a negotiation, so embrace these encounters and wield them as opportunities to learn and grow. It's not just about the destination, but the journey and every step you take towards becoming a more adept and emotionally intelligent negotiator.

www.ingramcontent.com/pod-product-compliance
Lightning Source LLC
Chambersburg PA
CBHW051536240526
45471CB00020B/3019